A Penny For Your Thoughts

Georgjana Hawks

BookLeaf
Publishing

India | USA | UK

Presentation by *BookLeaf Publishing*

Web: www.bookleafpub.com

E-mail: info@bookleafpub.com

ISBN: 9789360946654

First edition 2024

*This book is dedicated to my family, friends,
and my english teachers, Mrs. Varsanyi,
and Miss. Perry!*

Stay Young Little Goat

A little goat formed from the womb.

His mother has blessed him with the sunshine
that lies within the deep depths of our
compelling, azure blue sky.

He is born to sweet milk and butterflies.

Dew filled grass that quenches his panging
hunger.

He is pulled in by nature, and its verdurous,
comforting vines that hug around him
Alas, he is cursed to face our ruinous world one
day, as many are.

Taken far from his mother.

Horns that had grown magnificently, his only
pride left, only to be cut off, leaving him
shameful, head down in desolation.

In one gleam, one flash, one moment, the
darkest shadow of death will cover him like a
blood-chilling blanket.

He will welcome the tight grip of demise, for
when he wakes, his horns shall be restored, and
he will raise his head triumphantly, no longer
weighed down by his mortification.

When death comes, you may be young, but you
will be wiser and older. For death is a
complicated thing. Many embrace it, as life was
a struggle. Many fight it, but most don't when
they see the heavenliness of death waiting for
them.

The little goat does not grapple with death, for
growing up brings new wisdom.

But growing up brings new hardships.

But for now, just for now

He is fresh, and new, so innocent and harmless.

Until the day his horns sprout up like green
chutes from him

He will no longer be comforted by the
condolence of nature.

Stay young little goat.

Wings That Aren't Attached

Birds have wings, and so do I.

But my wings aren't attached, and I let out a cry.

Because I have to come down to the ground, and
though I hope I never do, it's sadly, not up to
you.

I want to fly forever, high up in the air.

But my wings aren't attached, and it's not the
least bit fair.

When I mount the hoop, soaring above in the
sky, my wings reattach, and finally, I can fly.

Or when the silk runs through my fingers, and I
wrap myself up tight, my wings rejoin me, and
once again, I can soar across the sky.

Wings that don't stay there are the greatest
sadness there can be, because when you feel like
flying, you are trapped, not free.

I do not wish to be a bird, but I do want my wings. For when my wings are attached I can finally flee.

When my wings are attached I am, me.

The Hidden Things

A dandelion sprouts up from the beaten Earth.

Its beautiful amber petals reach up to the aureate sun.

It may seem like the most resplendent flower to blossom in the world.

But, as many know, a dandelion is not what it seems. It is a weed, poison to the Earth and its soil.

A dandelion may as well not be called a dandelion or a flower, but instead, a Venus fly trap. It lures its victims in with its beauty and its ability to be whatever you wish.

That is, until the petals die and fall off. The beauty is gone, and you can see what is on the inside.

Not a flower of enchantment, that will blossom your heart, but a rotten plant that will invade and cause your heart to become filled with toxic hate.

Though the wildflower may wriggle its way into your heart, all hope is not lost.

When the veil of disguise falls, and you can see it for what it truly is, you can blow it away.

Just like that, just blow it away into the wind, do not let it poison your soul, your mind, and your love. Simply, let it go, escape from the wrath of trickery, and put yourself at ease.

But, wait, hold on, some may think that this dandelion may be more important than it seems, but it's just a flower… right?

A Story Stuck Inside You

There is a story on the tip of your tongue, pushing against your teeth.

But no matter how hard you try, your mouth will not open. All you wish is to serenade this story upon not just the world, but the universe.

It's almost as if your words are locked inside your soul, trying to break down the walls. But the golden key is nowhere to be found, and the words inside echo in your mind, driving you crazy with the need of expressing your tale.

You will go to sleep hearing the words muttered in your ear, you will wake to the rooster screeching the lines of your story. And then one day, everything will click, the lock will be broken, the story set free.

Your heart will beat faster and faster, the blood in your body pumping vigorously, then, your mouth will open.

The words pour out rapidly, you can see the magic the words you say hold. Golden waves swirl around you, causing all the hairs on your arm to stand up straight.

In that moment, you see beautiful things, inexpressible things, things so ordinary that it makes them, unordinary.

A gushing waterfall, woosh woosh woosh, it's mysteriously beautiful, but can also consume and drown you in one heartbeat.

A simple tree, groooooan, groan, its branches and wood sigh and grumble as it moves in the wind.

A lustrous dragonfly, flap flap, its delicate wings raise it higher and higher, it is something so common, but so wondrous to see.

The common things we see each day, can be the most beautiful, and can form a story so majestic that you can see the magic fill the air as the words push out of you.

At last, when the words have been spoken, and your tongue swollen, you will find that the most replenishing feeling there is, is letting a tale loose.

For there is no reason for living if a story stays trapped inside you, you will find that everyone must let their story go eventually.

The Way I Feel About The Way We Feel

I feel happy

I feel sad

I feel mad

People tell you that emotions are bad.

But emotions are real, and they come with you,
it's a packaged deal.

Don't bottle them up and bury them deep inside,
or cry yourself to sleep each night.

This message is out there for those who believe
they should hide, when really they need to
express what they feel on the inside.

Though your scars may seem unsightly, they are
more beautiful than you think. For there is no
reason to be miserable and pour yourself a drink.
Instead, take a pen, and dip it into a pot of ink.

Write out your emotions, stab the paper if you
need, till the page is filled with bleeding black
ink. You will find that your feelings don't weigh
you down anymore, you can finally leave that
big potato sack at the door.

No matter what sensation takes over you, always
know that you can push through.

Don't let your feelings take over your life, and
don't let them cut through you like a knife.

But it does you no good to store them away,
because they will come back to haunt you
someday.

Nevertheless, there is only one thing that
matters…

Don't ever let someone tell you that emotions
are bad, because emotions are something that we
are all born to have had.

Rain That Cleanses The Soul

The sky opens as wide as a smile, and the clouds burst with sweet-tasting dew.

This is where my ode to the rains begins.

I dance in the rain barefooted, I throw up my hands to celebrate the rain that cleanses the soul.

Though the rain washes the dirt off my feet, it also causes my feet to become unclean.

For the rain's cleanliness is a complicated thing.

The rain fills up the brook by the old house in the woods. The rain fills my heart with the wisdom that it holds.

When the rain patters down in delicate drops, you can hear the rain whisper a nursery rhyme that will sing you off to sleep.

People will go outside in the sunny weather, but never experience the water. The water that pours from the sky, and cleanses the Earth and its life.

People hide away, they do not realize, the rain is no ordinary thing, it is something whimsical, and only the wise can hear it sing.

When the raindrops cease to fall, the Earth will be born anew. Its cleansing is finished, and it is almost brand new.

There is a distinctive smell when you step outside. The rain has left your world smelling fresh, and the birds harmonize with the salty wind.

The rain brings new, without it, we would be trapped in a world of sweltering heat, in day, in night, there would be no more peace.

When the sky opens wide as a smile, and the clouds grow dark and heavy, you know the wet weather is coming. Do not hide away inside, instead, embrace the sugared sky.

If you listen close enough, you will hear each drizzle whisper the magic that goes unheard.

A Leisurely Walk To The End Of The World

I walk along the old, cracked sidewalk, when she comes up to me.

What are you doing? she asks.

I am on a leisurely walk to the end of the world.

The end of the world! There is no such thing!

And why not?

Well, I can see you have a bright imagination.

I have come to believe that imagination and reality are the same thing.

The same thing?! I am quite sure that I am right to believe that imagination and reality are opposites!

But imagination is a type of reality.

Imagination is fake, and reality is real!

Well, I am really walking to the end of the
world. But, I imagined that it is leisurely.

That doesn't make any sense, the whole situation
is made up to begin with!

Is it?

All you have managed to do is reach the end of
the sidewalk!!

Yes, I have reached the end of the world.

A Death That Comes Easily

You may find that one day, when you go over to your friend's house, she has a new toy. When you see that, you will naturally want it. You will become jealous.

But, if death suddenly came upon your friend, you would not want the same for you. Why is that?

The answer is simple: No one wishes for death. No one waits for it to show up on their doorstep, hoping for it to come and take them away.

Except, there is one teensy little issue with that uncomplicated answer. Life is certainly not uncomplicated, life is very much, complicated.

Which leads to the problem, some welcome death.

I know it sounds crazy, but it's true!

Unless the one reading this poem is one that understands, death is not something to fear, it just means your temporary end.

Of course, if that's not you, it will be soon. It's hard to comprehend and accept, but soon you will learn of the death that comes easily.

Now, there are two ways that explain the death that comes easily. The first is why people live in petrification, knowing that death will take them one day. The other way will show you how those very few people out there in the world know of the death that comes easily.

Though, isn't it peculiar, how one thing can mean so many different things? The death that comes easily means the trepidation of death, but also its opposite!
The fear, and the acceptance of death.

The fear of death mainly comes from one thing, even if you don't realize it.

It's not leaving your friends or family, it's not losing your possessions, it's not even about what happens to you after you die!

It's all about the unknown.

Yes, the unknown.

You do not know how, or when, or where you will die. If it will be easy and painless, or quite different.

And the part that leaves us pondering over death is that we don't know what it's like. How it feels, what we will be thinking, if we will know that it's happening, it's all unknown.

The fear of the unknown is the greatest fear there is.

You could be eating your morning breakfast, and choke on a raisin.

Maybe you're going for a swim, but you never leave the water.

What if you simply got a heart attack out of nowhere, and were gone?

I know, it's hard to think about, knowing that the unknown could happen at any time, the very fear could ruin your life.

But there is also a part of death that comes easily, that has a good side, the easy part to it.

When you spend enough time thinking about death, you might finally realize… death will always come, no matter what, there is nothing you can do.

Although it's a struggle to stay positive sometimes, you must think: Why am I even alive if all I worry about is dying?

It's a life of a cruel revolving circle. Be born into the world, think about, and fear death your entire life, then die.

It will take some longer than others, but one day you will have to realize that death is something that comes easily, as long as you let it. In most cases, dying can be easier than living sometimes.

Don't give up on life, but don't give up on death either. It is something you will always fear, and you can't help it. But, if you learn of the death that comes easily, you won't have to worry so much about your dying future, and instead focus on your wonderful present life!

Walking In Devilish Angel Shoes

I walk outside in my new shoes.

I feel important, I feel powerful, I feel invigorating.

The name-brand on my shoes labels me as more important.

The social status of what we wear and what we look like.

And as I walk outside, and the sun radiates its feverish waves on me and my shoes, something extraordinary occurs.

When the daylight hits my shoes they flash so bright that they could sizzle your eyes like eggs in a frying pan.

That's when I knew, I was walking in angel shoes.

They were perfectly white, they might have even had wings. All I knew was that I was at least floating a few inches off the ground.

I was the most marvelous angel there could be, until I fell.

Fell down, down, down, into the mud, mud, mud. I fell like the angels fall, kicked out of heaven, now a demon working for the loathed devil himself.

It was not the mud that caused the shoes to become so devilish. It was the fact that I finally realized that they were just some shoes.

Shoes that you walk in, shoes that you run in, shoes that you crease, shoes that you get muddy!

All shoes do is protect your feet, they should not be used for reaching a higher status!

Every time I wear those devilish angel shoes, I know that they are just, some shoes.

They will never be more, and they never should be.

Simplicity That's Not Simple

The first sip of that iced coffee. The maple brown liquid sliding down your throat, the ice chilling your tongue. Frost fogging the side of the cup. As it melts, it drips, drips, drips down onto your hand.

Everything about drinking an iced coffee is so simple, but yet, it can be one of the most captivating experiences.

Or going on an adventure, not sure where you're heading, all you know is that you're moving towards opportunity.

All you're doing is letting fate lead you on a journey, it's something that is almost too easy to do. But, it can lead to life-changing events that can bring you into happiness, tears, maybe even a new home.

Taking a hot shower, the water pouring down your back, wrapping around you like a heated blanket. It cleans you, and de-stresses you. When you step out of the steamy shower your

muscles are relaxed and unclenched, not like
how they were before, strained and aching.

All you have to do is turn on the water and walk
into the shower. Yet, it can do wonders for a
person.

Something as simple as receiving a hug from a
loved one can give you hope and relief. It can
make your whole day!

Just that warm fuzzy feeling of knowing that
someone loves you and feels for you. It comforts
you as you breathe in the positive emotions from
them, and let the negative ones go.

Things we do every day in life are so
extraordinary, but we don't even realize it. We
don't stop sometimes in life, and just enjoy how
wonderful everything is.

People are known to rush. Rush to work, rush
home, rush to get food, rush to school, no time
to stop and smell the flowers. They also tend to
rush through life.

Sometimes it's important to take a step back and
appreciate the un-simplicity in the simpleness of
what we do every day.

Secrecy Of The Dendrophile Poets In The World

At the forest's edge, you can see the line that separates the world from the wood.

Lush, emerald leaves reach outwards, like arms waiting for embrace. The roots hold the tree resolutely to the world. The strength of the outreaching roots will support me too.

A tree is an introvert as much as it is an extrovert.

The tree thrives as birds make their refuge in the mahogany branches. Little girls climb, and pick the scrumptious, fever red, apples.

Have you ever noticed how everything that belongs to the tree reaches out? The branches, the leaves, the roots, it's inviting you in.

Yet, it also stands in solitude, strong and hard. If the tree was soft it would fall to the ground in enfeeblement.

It is rooted to the forest, where most of the time
its company is only the birds that nest.

When you walk into a forest, it's almost as if you
have a secret to keep now. You have pledged
your loyalty to the nature the trees hide within.

For trees are protesters, gatekeepers of the
woodland. Once you have entered their fortress
you will wish to stay forever.

When the time comes to leave, you somehow
know deep inside that it is your duty to keep
your secret, and in turn, the forest will keep
yours.

It is almost impossible to leave the forest
without experiencing the feeling of being
dendrophile.

You will become a poet who holds the secrecy of
the forest, and whenever you search inside you,
you will always discover that the feeling of
being dendrophile is still, and will always be in
you.

The Storm That They Said Was Coming

A golden sky filled with tears summons the rainbow.

With pale, misty colors it arches across the sky. White flowers fall, almost as if announcing the kiss of love between the two.

If you look out the window, you have been born into a detective's tale.
Black and white almost, but you mustn't forget the golden hour that is shining in the atmosphere.

You can hear each trickle as raindrops fall, cleansing the Earth, washing the dirt off your feet.

That had said a storm was coming, but all that really came was magic. Magic and beauty that fills you with hope and imagination.

For is a storm ever really a storm, but instead, an experience?

Musical Moments

Music, vocal or instrumental sounds combined in such a way as to produce beauty of form, harmony, and expression of emotion.

Music, what you listen to when you work out at the gym.

Music, blasting in your ears when you're walking to school.

Music, playing in the background as you work on homework or a business project.

Music motivates us.

If you close your eyes for just one minute, whether you're listening or creating music, you'll find the spark.

You raise your hands up high, almost as if you were the one conducting the music. You'll rise from your seat, and dance.

It doesn't matter if you're a good or bad dancer, you'll pour your heart out, and lay it all on the floor where you will twirl and spin and stomp all over it.

Music is in all of us, and it sparks imagination and emotions.

We all have our favorite song, our sad song, our mad song, that one song that you pretend you hate because everyone else does, but you actually really love it.

We take music for granted, when really, our whole lives revolve around it!

Each day holds so many musical moments from the second you wake up, to the instance you close your eyes.

Everything is making music: the birds singing, that little boy across the street banging pots and pans, even your washing machine!

Anything can be music if you listen for the spark.

If you look for the musical moments in life you are sure to find them, because music was made to reach out to people, not hide away.

If you want to hear the music, you will.

A Murderer's Guide To A Rainbow

Red, the color that fills my head.

When I am sleeping, when I'm awake, all I see is red.

The color of blood, the color of my hands, the color of the knife I hide under the bed.

Orange, it represents my pride.

The pride I have to kill if I want to be a killer. I know all too well that you get caught when you act like an arrogant peacock.

Strutting around, showing off your feathers… makes it easy for hunters to spot you.

Yellow, like a lemon.

Most think that lemons are sour, but some dig right in.

Funny how you can turn something so sour into something so sweet.

Unless, of course, it's just the sugar they added
to the lemonade to disguise the sour taste.

Green, it's what everyone wishes to be, except
me.

The good guys are green, you can go when the
stop light turns green, green is the color of the
grass, the trees, green is the color of everything.

But green will never touch me, it will shrivel to
a crisp, ugly brown.

Green cannot take over me.

Blue, the sadness that I hide.

I am lonely, a murderer is not used to company.

But we killers must be stone-faced and
stone-hearted, or we won't survive our lives,
blue is the color that I hide inside.

Purple, my power.

I am royalty, king and queen of them all, the best
slayer there is.

I enjoy wielding the power that I have, purple is
my favorite color.

The more power you have, the longer you stay
alive.

I plan on staying alive for a long time.

A Long Line Of Corruption

Long live the queen! Long live the queen!

I hear them ranting, I hear them screaming! I hear them in my head! I feel like dying on the inside, my heart is aching! But I have to keep my nerve, I have a kingdom to run, I must act ladylike, oh, how I wish I had been a son.

Long live the queen! Long live the queen!

A child is born, of course a girl. For as a princess is born each time, they are all cursed to be wrapped into the chains of the never-ending circle of life and death, the never-ending line of hopelessness queens.

Long live the queen! Long live the queen!

I must endure the pain as the queen, of taking on a husband, ruling your kingdom, and raising a young princess. I am forced to teach my beloved child the values that are unwillingly forced into a lady's mind.

Long live the queen! Long live the queen!

Death will come for me, but my daughter now must face the painfulness of being a queen, and going on with the cruel cycle of life.

We must celebrate! We must celebrate! A new queen rules!

I am a new queen, but I do not believe I am new to this life. My mother has taught me the restrictions of being a lady. I just don't get why the females in this world are on such short leashes! I myself plan to be a brave and righteous leader to my kingdom.

Long live the queen! Long live the queen!

I thought my mother had taught me everything I needed to know, but I am dying on the inside. Life is not what it promised to be, I hope death is. Nevertheless, I am in a position where I can not make the decision to end the brutal circle.

Long live the queen! Long live the queen!

A child is born, of course a girl. For as a princess is born each time, they are all cursed to be wrapped into the chains of the never-ending circle of life and death, the never-ending line of hopelessness queens.

Long live the queen! Long live the queen!

I wish nothing more than to stay away from my young child's mind. But, she is a princess, and will continue the line of royalty, continue the circle. As words come out of my mouth, I only think about death.

We must celebrate! We must celebrate! A new queen rules!

I never wished to be born with royalty in my blood. I never wanted to be queen. My mother taught "all I needed to know," but I want to know more. I have just begun my reign, and I expect it to be torturing. A long line of unhappy queens, accepting life for what it is. Well I'm different.

Long live the queen! Long live the queen!

As I had expected, life is as I thought it would be. I am miserable, tired, fed up, and angry. How, how could this line of cruelty continue on? They say it is a queen's job to do, yet they have never been rulers themselves. I know I am different, for everyone before me, mother, grandmother, grandmother's mother, and even further than that, they have all been miserable, and I'm going to save the future princesses.

Long live the queen! Long live the queen!

There is no marriage, no child is born. There is no new princess, even when the queen's death comes.

There is… no queen?

The circle has been broken, the cursed princesses and queens are finally at peace.

Time Machine

Your parents talk about how lucky you are to live in the world you live in today.

All the new and fancy technology, the education you receive, the home you live in.

But yet, we still strive for more. Flying cars, robots that deliver food, advanced phones.

Our race will never be happy with what we have, until there is nothing left to have. Have you ever thought that maybe what we really need… is less?

Imagine you have a time machine that can take you back to the past. Anywhere in the past, your parent's time, medieval times, even ancient Greek times!

Everything would seem so, unreal. Living in one-room cabins, tending to farm animals instead of going to school, writing on chalkboard slates.

Or maybe as you're walking down the path you
see a knight heading towards a castle, a poet
sitting on a wall singing out his noble words.
Maybe you meet a princess, fair and beautiful,
but ready to pull out a sword at any moment and
join her parent's army.

Women with golden leaf crowns, and
snow-white robes. Men wearing heavy armor,
weighed down by the metal and their hidden fear
of war.

Handsome horses dripping in chainmail,
bloodthirsty battles that result in great victories
and devastating losses.

When you come back to our present time, it
doesn't seem that exciting anymore. You're
almost jealous of the people back then.

They got to experience so much more than you
did, and yes, you are thankful to be home, safe
and comfortable.

But with your time machine you have the chance
to realize what most people don't, people are
moving too fast, they keep pushing forward
without looking back to see what destruction
they've caused.

There is so much treasure in the past left to explore and find, but we risk forgetting about all of the little things in it when we start moving too fast.

Sure, you'll always have the chance to learn about the big wars, and the famous generals, indians, royalty, ect.

But, what about the small details, like maybe there was a Princess Adelaide, she was born a hunter, her father gifted her a bow and arrow when she was eight.

When she grew to be sixteen she no longer had the choice to do whatever she wanted, she was forced to obey the rules and act like a lady. But she never listened anyway.

Or maybe there was a boy named Arthur, he lived with his mom out on a farm.

All he wanted to do was paint. But his mom thought that he would become poor if that was all he made out of his life.

Arthur would not give up though, with each stroke of his paintbrush, his soul became more lively.

He painted the whole countryside, and when his mother saw it, she was astounded at how beautiful it was.

The faster we run away from the past, the more we will lose, the future awaits, but the past should not be overlooked.

When The Heart Is Broken
The Shards Kill

I saw your friends at the bar last night, and I know those tears were fake.

You told them that I broke your heart, but what they don't know…

Is that I didn't break your heart, you tore mine apart.

You thought that once you tore my heart out I'd be broken, dead. But little did you know, I'm here to stand all on my own.

We aren't sheep following the shepherd all around, we're wolves now, no more, "safe and sound."

You lied to me, told me that I was protected by your staff, but little did I know that your protection would hurt me so much.

I wince at the touch.

It hurt me so much.

The women of our world are forced to follow on
a leash, stay in the men's shadow, let him
discipline you as he pleases.

The queen is forced by law, she must marry the
king she first saw.

She is forced to hide the shed of her tears.

Until midnight, when she murders the king,
takes control of the land. People think she's
crazy as more and more men ask for her hand..
But she refuses.

When her subjects found out what she had done,
they prepared to burn her at the stake, there was
nowhere to run.

As the ember flames reached towards the wood,
she realized that she had to speak, so that her
murderess actions would not always be
misunderstood.

She raised her voice and spoke out:

My people, I understand that you think I am evil

I'm not denying that I murdered your king.

But just listen to me, for one moment, you will see!

The law forces me to marry a man of royalty.

I must stand, "happily," in his shadow, as he runs his kingdom.

The women are never valued, they are there to look weak, to be rescued by men, and for them to keep.

The men that we run away from, they will say that it was your fault, that you broke their hearts, but really, they ripped yours apart.

The women of this world are overlooked, we are abused, and then re-used.

My fellow subjects, have you ever heard of a queendom, I think not!

But we could make it known, if you stand with me, and give me back the throne!

I will not stand down anymore, as the male race takes us for advantage, they say we can not be warriors… but we are stronger than all of them!

The queen never was burned that night, and the women started up quite the big fight.

The men did not approve, sounds like them, but they were left in solitude. The women were not trapped by their spells anymore, some even walked straight out the door.

Gender should not defy how we are treated, the men have been defeated, but they will not give up, the women still have to struggle through life sometimes.

But we have each other, and even when you are forced to follow the rules, dress appropriately, wear a dress, cover your shoulders so you don't distract the boys, you know that you are always a warrior, even if you can't show them by dressing it, they'll find out soon enough.

Poets Quills Break Easily

Edgar Allan Poe, William Shakespeare, Emily
Dickinson, all breathtaking poets and writers.

It's heartbreaking to see how easily technology
can break their inspiring pieces of art.

All you have to do is go onto your phone and
ask AI to continue they're poems, and that's that.

But AI cannot just steal they're hard work and
dedication, they have worked tirelessly to create
words that will lift the world to greater heights.

People have thoughts, feelings, emotions.
Robots are just designed to be humankind's
servant. They do what they are told, and their
words have no meaning.

A poet's work can be shattered just by one
crack, their words are powerful but fragile.

With one click of a button, we can destroy some
of the most moving poems ever written.

Don't Let It Take Control

There is always a hero and a villain in every
book.

The beautiful princess and the evil witch.

The monster and the man.

But what the fairytale world doesn't know, is
that there is never a hero.

All the mighty warriors, the elegant queens,
none of them are the good guys.

The villains could be heroes if they wanted to,
the heroes could be villains. Nothing is stopping
them but their own will.

Every hero has it inside of them. The villain is
always wanting out, there's no controlling it.

They are all merely just villains posing as
heroes, trying to hide what's on the inside.

It's running through their mind all day, all night,
they hear it in them in every battle they fight.

Don't let it.

Don't let it.

Don't let it.

Don't let it take over my mind, and my soul, don't let it take control.

Don't let it take control.

Don't let it take… control.

In that second there is no longer a hero standing before you, but a monster.

They are willing to kill in a moment, they don't stop or they'd be dead, if they are satisfied then they are already dead.

Once it's taken control, there is no escaping. It has claimed you since the second you gave in.

There are no real heroes, just villains in disguise.. And they will all take control, eventually.

The Pain of Fear

47

A red hot sting spreads up your arm, the bee's sting has pierced your skin.

The bee is dead, lying on the ground, limp.

Beautiful Scribbles

Anyone can write.

But how do you write?

Did you buy old scroll paper so you could pretend that you are from medieval times? Did you spend your days up in your treehouse, writing stories about your adventures, and love letters to the princess?

Do you write on your computer each morning with a fresh cup of coffee, working on that new book that you are hoping to publish?

Do you write textbooks to help people learn and grow? Do you spend your time wondering about how your writing is going to help the world?

Do you gift your writing to people? Do you help inspire them, and make them feel like someone cares about them?

Do you journal each night, and fill the pages with scribbles that no one can read but you, and only you know how special those words are?

Anyone can write, but what is important is that you can express yourself.

Anyone can write.

Anyone can write a book.

Anyone can be a poet.

www.ingramcontent.com/pod-product-compliance
Lightning Source LLC
LaVergne TN
LVHW050941200726
843508LV00011B/2405